Tell Me – Tell Me More...
Amazing Animals A to Z

Linda Wong, Author

Tina Stergios, Illustrator

3G Publishing, Inc.
Loganville, Ga 30052
www.3gpublishinginc.com
Phone: 1-888-442-9637

©2020 Linda Wong, Las Vegas, Nevada, USA. All rights reserved.

First Published by 3G Publishing, Inc.   March, 2020

Printed in the United States of America

ISBN: 9781941247716 (Hardcover)
ISBN: 9781941247679 (Softcover)
ISBN: 9781941247662 (E-book)
ISBN: 9781941247686 (Activity Book)

Illustrations by Tina Stergios

No part of this book may be reproduced, stored in a retrieval system,
or transmitted by any means without the written permission of the author.

Tell Me- Tell Me More....
www.TellMe-TellMeMore.com

Dedication

I dedicate this book to my grandchildren Makai, Kalia, Mailee, and Koa. They represent the many children who enjoy learning and having fun!

I also dedicate this book to all the parents, teachers, and adults who introduce children to the wonders of reading and share with children the joy of learning. I commend you for promoting reading and engaging in the process of educating all children.

TELL ME – TELL ME MORE
Amazing Animals A to Z

TABLE of CONTENTS

Ants	What would it be like to have hundreds of brothers and sisters?	1
Bear	What is different about the way you and bears eat and sleep?	2
Camel	What would be difficult about living in a desert?	3
Dolphin	What do you think dolphins eat under water?	4
Elephant	Why should you be careful standing next to an elephant?	5
Fox	How are foxes and dogs different?	6
Gorilla	How do you think gorillas carry food to their nests?	7
Hummingbird	Why do hummingbirds fly to warmer weather in the winter?	8
Iguana	What would you do if you saw an iguana basking in the sun?	9
Jellyfish	Why should you avoid touching a live jellyfish?	10
Kangaroo	What things would you do if you could hop or leap thirty feet?	11
Lion	How are lions and lionesses different from each other?	12
Moose	What part of a moose would you see when it swims in a river?	13
Newt	How could a newt's body parts get injured, damaged, or torn off?	14
Octopus	What things could you do if you had eight arms?	15
Penguin	How are penguins different from other kinds of birds?	16
Quail	How could hunters use dogs to get quail to fly?	17
Raccoon	Why are raccoons also called masked bandits?	18
Skunk	Why should you back away slowly if you see a skunk?	19
Turtle	Why and where do you like to hide?	20
Umbrellabird	What kind of food could an umbrellabird find in treetops?	21
Vulture	What dead animals in an open field might a vulture eat?	22
Woodpecker	How fast can you tap your fingers on a table twenty times?	23
X-ray tetra	What would you see if you could see through your skin?	24
Yak	What would it be like to have long hair that touches the ground?	25
Zebra	What animals without stripes does a zebra look like to you?	26

a-a-ants

Tell me, ants. Tell me, ants.
Where are you going?

We are going to our underground home.
We follow scented trails so we do not get lost.
We bring food to the ants in our colony.

Tell me more.
You can find us in trees, in plants,
under rocks, or in ant hills.

We carry itsy bitsy seeds, leaves,
and insects in our jaws.

Our mother, the queen, has hundreds
of baby ants every day.

What would it be like to have hundreds of brothers and sisters?

b-b-bear

Tell me, bear. Tell me, bear.
When do you sleep?

In the summer, I only take naps.
In the winter, I sleep all day and all night.
I sleep in dens, in caves, or between rocks.

Tell me more.
I eat plants, fish, farm crops,
and dead animals.

The food I eat during the summer
is stored as fat.

The stored fat nourishes my body
during the winter.

What is different about the way you and bears eat and sleep?

c-c-camel

Tell me, camel. Tell me, camel.
What is inside the hump on your back?

I store body fat inside my hump.
The body fat is processed into water.
I can live months without eating or drinking.

Tell me more.
I am used to transport people and
    cargo in the desert.

I shut my nostrils during sand storms.

My three eyelids protect my eyes
    from blowing sand.

What would be difficult about living in a desert?

d-d-dolphin

Tell me, dolphin. Tell me, dolphin.
Why is there a hole in the top of your head?

I use the blowhole to breathe.
I blow out old air and breathe in fresh air.
I cannot breathe under water.

Tell me more.

I use my flippers to steer my body.
My tail fin helps me swim fast.
I swim with a group of dolphins
   called a pod.

What do you think dolphins eat under water?

e-e-elephant

Tell me, elephant. Tell me, elephant.
Why do you have a trunk?

I use my trunk to put food and water in my mouth.
I use my trunk to spray water on my body.
I use my trunk to breathe.

Tell me more.
I eat branches, bark, fruit, and grass.
I am the biggest animal that lives on land.
I flap my big ears to cool my
   huge body.

Why should you be careful standing next to an elephant?

f-f-fox

Tell me, fox. Tell me, fox.
Why do you hide in your den?
I hide in my den to surprise my prey.
I crouch down before I jump out to attack.
I eat animals, birds, and reptiles.

Tell me more.
I walk on my toes.
I shed my thick fur or pelt every year.
When threatened, I growl, bark, and howl.

How are foxes and dogs different?

g-g-gorilla

Tell me, gorilla. Tell me, gorilla.
> *Do you walk on your hands?*

I walk on my knuckles and on my feet.
My arms are longer than my legs.
I am a very intelligent primate.

Tell me more.
> My family group is called a troop.
> I socialize, play and groom others in my troop.
> I communicate by making different sounds.

How do you think gorillas carry food to their nests?

h-h-hummingbird

Tell me, hummingbird. Tell me, hummingbird.
Do you hum?

I do not hum like you hum.
My wings beat very fast and make a humming sound.
I can fly forward, backward or stay in place.

Tell me more.
I use my long beak to drink nectar in flowers.
I have bright iridescent colored feathers.
I am the smallest bird in the world.

Why do hummingbirds fly to warmer weather in the winter?

i-i-iguana

Tell me, iguana. Tell me, iguana.
> *Are you a small dinosaur?*

No, I am a large lizard with spikes on my back.
I bob my head up and down.
I whip my long tail back and forth.

Tell me more.
I use my size, tail, and claws to protect myself.
I use my tail to swim to escape predators.
I can regrow my tail if it gets pulled off.

What would you do if you saw an iguana basking in the sun?

j - j - jellyfish

Tell me, jellyfish. Tell me, jellyfish.
Are you really made from jelly?

No, but my bell (top) feels like jelly but is not jelly.

My bell gets big and small, and big and small.

This is how I push myself through the water.

Tell me more.

I live in the ocean, but I am not a fish.

My tentacles can sting my prey and people.

The waves sometimes push me onto a beach.

Why should you avoid touching a live jellyfish?

k-k-kangaroo

Tell me, kangaroo. Tell me, kangaroo.
How do you use you strong back legs?

I use my strong back legs to hop and jump fast.

I can lean back on my tail to kick with my back legs.

I move slowly when I walk on all four legs.

Tell me more.

Baby kangaroos are called joeys.

The joeys ride in a pouch on the mother's belly.

Joeys jump out to eat grass and plants.

What things would you do if you could hop or leap thirty feet?

l - l - lion

Tell me, lion. Tell me, lion.
> *Why do you not go hunting for food?*

I stay home to protect the cubs in our family.

I cannot move fast because of my heavy mane.

The smaller, faster females (lionesses) do the hunting.

Tell me more.

I eat deer, zebra, buffalo, and giraffe.

I also eat leftovers of animals killed by other animals.

You can hear me roar loudly for miles.

How are lions and lionesses different from each other?

m - m - moose

Tell me, moose. Tell me, moose.
Do your antlers ever fall off?

I shed my antlers every year.

Only the male moose (bulls) have antlers.

After they fall off, bigger antlers grow.

Tell me more.

I have a great sense of smell and hearing.

I have bad eyesight.

I eat plants, pinecones, bark, and shrubs.

What part of a moose would you see when it swims in a river?

n-n-newt

Tell me, newt. Tell me, newt.
> *Do you live in water and on land?*

I hatch from an egg in water.

I become a tadpole with gills.

I move to live on land when I grow legs, lungs, and a tail.

Tell me more.

As an adult, I return to the water to lay eggs.

I eat worms, snails, beetles, crickets, and insects.

I can regrow my legs, tail, and other body parts if they get torn off or injured.

How could a newt's body parts get injured, damaged, or torn off?

o - o - octopus

Tell me, octopus. Tell me, octopus.
　　How do you protect yourself from sharks?

I squirt black ink to confuse my enemies.

I push water out of my head to jet propel away.

I change the color of my skin so I am hard to see.

Tell me more.

I use my eight arms to crawl on the
　　ocean floor.

I have no bones so I can squeeze
　　into small spaces.

I can regrow my arms if
　　they get torn off.

What things could you do if you had eight arms?

p-p-penguin

Tell me, penguin. Tell me, penguin.
Are you really a bird?

I am a bird, but I cannot fly.

I stand up straight and waddle on my two feet.

I use my wings as flippers to swim in icy water.

Tell me more.

My belly is covered with white feathers.

My back and wings have layers of black feathers.

I hold my breath when I dive under water for food.

How are penguins different from other kinds of birds?

q-q-quail

Tell me, quail. Tell me, quail..
Where do you live?
I live in fields, low grassy areas, and bushes.
I am a game bird that prefers to run, not fly.
Young quail hatch from eggs in ground nests.

Tell me more.
My plume of feathers bobs when I run fast.
I scratch the soil for seeds and insects to eat.
I fear coyotes, foxes, owls, hawks, and snakes.

How could hunters use dogs to get quail to fly?

r-r-raccoon

Tell me, raccoon. Tell me, raccoon.

Are you a troublemaker?

Yes, I roam around at night and cause mischief.

I raid garbage cans and damage buildings.

I destroy gardens and crops.

Tell me more.

I have a black, furry mask around my eyes.

I have black rings around my bushy tail.

I can spread diseases to people and animals.

Why are raccoons sometimes called masked bandits?

s - s - skunk

Tell me, skunk. Tell me, skunk.
> *Do you squirt a stinky odor?*

Yes, I lift my tail and spray as far as ten feet.

My stinky odor protects me from enemies.

I hiss, growl, and spit when I am threatened.

Tell me more.

I have one or two white stripes on my
    back and tail.

I roam around mostly at night.

I have good hearing and smell,
    but poor eyesight.

Why should you back away slowly if you see a skunk?

t - t - turtle

Tell me, turtle. Tell me, turtle.
Where do you live?
I live in lakes, rivers, and ponds.
I move slowly on land or when I climb on logs.
I move to mud or sand to dig holes to lay eggs.

Tell me more.
I stick my nose out of the water to breathe.
My hard shell protects me.
I can hide by pulling my head and feet inside the shell.

Why and where do you like to hide?

u-u-umbrellabird

Tell me, umbrellabird. Tell me, umbrellabird.
Can you fly?

I am a large bird so flying is hard for me to do.

I live high in tropical rainforest treetops.

I perch on branches and hop from tree to tree.

Tell me more.

I have a crest of feathers on the top of my head.

I have a pouch (wattle) that hangs from my throat.

I inflate my waddle to make loud calls to other birds.

What kind of food could an umbrellabird find in treetops?

v-v-vulture

Tell me, vulture. Tell me, vulture.
Do you eat dead animals?

Yes, I am a scavenger.

I fly in circles with other vultures.

I feed on carcasses but do not eat the bones.

Tell me more.

I have large wings and can fly for a long time.

I use my good eyesight to spot dead animals.

I also use my good sense of smell to find food.

What dead animals in an open field might a vulture eat?

w-w-woodpecker

Tell me, woodpecker. Tell me, woodpecker.
> *Why do you tap and peck on trees?*

I tap or peck fast to remove tree bark.

I find ants, beetles, and insects under the bark.

I make noise when I peck on poles and fences.

Tell me more.

I use stiff tail feathers to keep my balance when I peck.

I point my toes forward and backward for a good grip.

I use my long, sticky tongue to eat seeds, lick sap, and catch flies.

How fast can you tap your fingers on a table twenty times?

x-x-x-ray tetra

Tell me, x-ray tetra. Tell me, x-ray tetra.

How are you like x-ray?

I have transparent, "see-through" skin.

I have a small, flat body.

You can see my backbone and organs.

Tell me more.

I am a freshwater fish in the Amazon River.

I also am raised for fish tanks or aquariums.

I lay 300-400 eggs that hatch in 24 hours.

What would you see if you could see through your skin?

Y - y - yak

Tell me, yak. Tell me, yak.
  How do you survive in cold regions?

My long, shaggy hair touches the ground.

It keeps me warm like a blanket.

My large horns break through the ice for food.

Tell me more.

I live in herds in high, cold regions of Asia.

In lower regions, I am domesticated or trained.

I pull plows and carry loads through the mountains.

What would it be like to have long hair that touches the ground?

z - z - zebra

Tell me, zebra Tell me, zebra.
Are you stripes black or white?
I have white stripes on my black body fur.
Every zebra has a different stripe pattern.
I live in Africa in herds or harems.

Tell me more.
I communicate by making different sounds.

The direction my ears point shows my mood.

I run zig zag patterns to escape from predators.

What animals without stripes does a zebra look like to you?

www.ingramcontent.com/pod-product-compliance
Lightning Source LLC
Chambersburg PA
CBHW061414090426
42742CB00023B/3467